Making the Grades

A Grouch-Free Guide to
Homeschool Grading

Lee Binz,
The HomeScholar

© 2018 by **The HomeScholar LLC**

All Rights Reserved. No part of this publication may be reproduced in any form or by any means, including scanning, photocopying, or otherwise without prior written permission of the copyright holder.

First Printing, 2015

Printed in the United States of America
Cover Design by Robin Montoya
Edited by Kimberly Charron

ISBN: 151163250X
ISBN-13: 978-1511632508

Disclaimer: Parents assume full responsibility for the education of their children in accordance with state law. College requirements vary, so make sure to check with the colleges about specific requirements for homeschoolers. We offer no guarantees, written or implied, that the use of our products and services will result in college admissions or scholarship awards.

Making the Grades

A Grouch-Free Guide to
Homeschool Grading

What are Coffee Break Books?

Making the Grades is part of The HomeScholar's Coffee Break Book series.

Designed especially for parents who don't want to spend hours and hours reading a 400-page book on homeschooling high school, each book combines Lee's practical and friendly approach with detailed, but easy-to-digest information, perfect to read over a cup of coffee at your favorite coffee shop!

Never overwhelming, always accessible and manageable, each book in the series will give parents the tools they need to tackle the tasks of homeschooling high school, one warm sip at a time.

Everything about these Coffee Break Books is designed to suggest simplicity, ease and comfort - from the size (fits in a purse), to the font and paragraph length (easy on the eyes), to the price (the same as a Starbucks Venti Triple Caramel Macchiato). Unlike a fancy coffee drink, however, these books are guilt-free pleasures you will want to enjoy again and again!

Table of Contents

What are Coffee Break Books? v
"Mom, Your Grades Are Bogus"..............................9
Grading With Tests..13
Grading Without Tests..17
How Great Schools Grade 21
How Great Teachers Grade 27
Grading Papers..33
Determining Class Grades 39
What About Weighting Grades? 47
Learning is More Important than Grades..............55
GPA Conversion Charts...57
The Annoyed Mom's Guide to Grading 63
The HomeScholar Answers Parents' Questions 75
Who is Lee Binz and What Can She Do for Me? ...91
Testimonials 93
Also From The HomeScholar... 97

Introduction

"Mom, Your Grades Are Bogus"

If you're like many homeschool parents, you stress a bit about grading your children's work, and wonder whether you can even give them valid grades. Does anyone take mommy grades seriously? Some homeschoolers don't like assigning grades at all, but it's important to remember that most colleges require them when a student applies for admission.

In this book, we'll cover different methods you can use in your homeschool to evaluate your students, both grade and non-grade based. As we begin, think back to when your children were little, and you used chore charts to evaluate whether they were meeting your expectations. By the time we're done, you'll see that grading in high school is an easy extension of the chore charts you used when your kids were little. We will use examples of syllabuses from different schools to see how different teachers grade. We'll cover grading with tests, written papers, work and assignments, and discuss how to put grades into a format that will make sense to you and how to determine grades for your child's transcript.

Our Homeschool

I didn't do much grading, even when my children were in high school. My sons even questioned the grades I gave on their papers and transcripts. My oldest son, Kevin, thought my homeschool grades were bogus. I know this because one day he told me, "Mom, your grades are bogus." Who's going to believe the grades my Mom gives me?" It's funny when your children tell you such things, because you just don't know how to respond! Fortunately, life experience came to the rescue.

During his last year of homeschooling, he took some classes at a community college and noticed a few things that surprised him. At the community college, professors told Kevin, "Don't worry about my syllabus because I know what grade you should be given, and no matter what my syllabus says, I'm going to make sure that you get the grade you deserve." This worried Kevin, since he's a bit of a perfectionist, and he never feels he deserves an *A*; he was worried the teacher would grade him too low.

Other professors gave credit for class attendance, participation, discussion, and homework. If students scored poorly on a test, they were allowed to "drop" one test. One teacher declared that the highest grade on each test would become "100 percent" and all the other students were graded on a sliding scale.

In other classes, if the average grade for a test was 75 percent, many professors declared 75 percent was an A, or added 25 points to everybody's test, thus grading on the curve. After he experienced the way community college professors graded, Kevin came back to me and said I was a much tougher grader! He finally realized mommy grades were legitimate! Mine were and yours are, too. Let's look at some ways to help the process be painless!

Chapter 1

Grading With Tests

Just as there are many ways to homeschool, there are different ways to evaluate your student's work. Most people use a combination of tests, homework, and writing, depending on the course being evaluated. I graded using tests for math, science, and foreign language because the curriculum I used included tests, but I didn't use tests for other classes. I was looking for mastery of each subject, not a certain percentage score, and this influenced how I assigned grades. Some families incorporate standardized tests to either replace or supplement the tests in their curriculum. If, for instance, your child takes the Iowa Test of Basic Skills or the

CAT (or even the PSAT or SAT), you could use the words in those tests as part of your evaluation.

There's no right way to evaluate your child! It's perfectly fine if you want to use the tests in your curriculum. You can administer them orally, as quizzes, or in a written format.

Valuable Skills

Test-taking skills are important to learn as your children get older. It's a good idea to expose kids to fill-in-the-bubble tests so they get comfortable with them. Fill-in-the-bubble tests are merely a part of life—like voting or taking a driver's test! Writing a short, handwritten essay is also an important test-taking skill that will help your child in the future. When your child applies for a job, employers might say, "Sit down and tell us a bit about yourself in writing." Learning to write a quick essay is important not only for a grade, but as a life skill as well.

The Purpose of Tests

If you are already aware of what your student knows in a subject, then tests become less valuable to you as a professional educator. If you consider why public schools use grades, remember they're evaluating 30 students at once. If they evaluated all of them orally, it would be utter chaos, so it makes a lot of sense for schools to grade using tests. They have to do so in order to efficiently evaluate what each student knows (not to mention maintain federal funding). As a homeschooler, you don't have those problems, and are not tied to using tests to determine what your child knows.

Even in your use of grades to evaluate your child, you have a lot of leeway. Grading in schools varies more widely than you can imagine! Even within the same school, grading is different from teacher to teacher. If you get a sample syllabus from several schools, you'll see some interesting approaches. Every school does it in a completely different way, and every teacher within each school can approach it differently, too. You can evaluate your student in your own unique ways.

Chapter 2

Grading Without Tests

When faced with courses such as math or spelling, most homeschool parents feel confident in their grading methods. But what about more challenging courses such as fine arts or creative writing—how do you grade those? If you were teaching culinary arts and your student had an assignment to create a yummy chocolate dessert, how would you grade it?

Mastery

While grades definitely have their place, an equally useful method of evaluating your child's education is using the concept of mastery. Mastery simply means your student has learned the things you want them to and are meeting your expectations.

Think about a chocolate dessert again. If you're grading a student's culinary arts class using the concept of mastery, you could use a variety of criteria to evaluate them. First, you might consider their work based on taste, and then you might evaluate them on the appearance of their work or presentation. You could grade them on a variety of things based on their overall mastery of culinary arts, all of which would be a part of their final grade.

Perfection

There's a huge difference between mastery and perfection. A great example of this would be my checkbook, because it looks like a bunch of chicken scratches. Sometimes I have to scratch out numbers and start subtracting and adding everything again, so my checkbook is not perfect. I do have mastery over addition, subtraction, multiplication, and division, but sometimes I make mistakes. Whether you're grading with or without tests, it's still important to remember that a grade of 100 percent does not have to mean perfection.

Meeting Expectations

If you're reviewing your student's test, you could send it back so they can correct anything wrong, or if you're correcting an English paper, you could circle the mistakes and ask the student to correct it. Both scenarios indicate that you have high expectations. If your child is meeting your high expectations, it's fine to give them 100 percent for their work. This is what I did most of the time; I gave my sons 100 percent based on something they knew, produced, or accomplished if they met my high expectations.

You can give a grade for intangibles such as oral presentations, classroom discussions, class participation, or finishing homework. Every time my sons completed a chapter of math, performed the end-of-chapter test, or finished all their homework, I gave them 100 percent. They worked hard for these grades and spent hours on math assignments each day, so I believed they earned a reward for all this work. In the end, mastery of important concepts is what you are seeking for your student.

Chapter 3

How Great Schools Grade

Many homeschool parents struggle to determine a good grading system for their high school students, so I'd like to share a little information with you that I think will be encouraging. In Seattle, there's a great private school called Lakeside School. Students of this prestigious place are said to go on to earn an average income of over $1.5 million a year. Of course, having Bill Gates and Paul Allen as alumni may skew those results a bit. Nevertheless, Lakeside is a great school, one of Seattle's best.

I looked at Lakeside's curriculum a while ago when I was trying to write a homeschool course description for a general class. I visited their website and looked up their course description for Physical Science Grade 9. I particularly wanted to see their grading criteria. According to the syllabus, grades are earned by accumulating points in several areas, including responsibility and participation in class activities. I had to chuckle at this, in light of my own homeschool experience. I don't think I ever gave my children a grade for responsibility or for participation.

Lakeside students are given points for homework assignments, but those points are based on turning in homework, not on its correctness. They are given grades for presentations, oral reports, quizzes, and unit tests. In order to get an *A* in the class, a student has to get an *A* in every category, which implies you can get 100 percent for responsibility, participation, homework assignments, presentation, quizzes, and unit tests.

The course description goes on to say that typical homework assignments might include reading articles, answering questions in the text, completing workshcets, writing a lab report, preparing presentations, studying the vocabulary, organizing materials, reading scientific journals, and researching information sources on the Internet. This is how a great school grades Physical Science Grade 9.

The next class I looked at was called Lodging Management. It was a class for 11th and 12th graders, and was one credit. If you feel a bit funny about some of the classes you're teaching, you should probably lighten up, knowing that Lakeside School teaches Lodging Management! You can be comfortable teaching any specialized class your child wants to take!

In this particular class, grading is based on a point system, and each student's points are added and divided by the total number of points possible. Grades come from daily work: quizzes, projects and tests. Here are some of the ways students were evaluated:

- 15 percent of their grade was based on being a "bell ringer." I looked hard but could not figure out what a bell ringer was. I think it had something to do with promptness, but I don't know for sure.

- 20 percent of their grade was for daily work and doing their homework

- 10 percent for quizzes

- 25 percent for tests

- 30 percent for projects

Only 35 percent of this class was based on any testing at all, while 65 percent of the class was based on evaluations other than tests. When you do use tests, you should also use other evaluation methods to make up your student's final grade. Great schools do it and you can, too.

On their website, Lakeside says 100 percent of their graduates are accepted and ultimately enrolled in four-year post-secondary institutions. This is also true of my own homeschool, and it can be true of your homeschool. Don't let grading intimidate you. It can be simple and straightforward.

Chapter 4

How Great Teachers Grade

Perhaps you're comfortable figuring out how to evaluate your child but you still doubt your ability to assign fair grades. Let's look at how a typical public school teacher does the job. My nephew teaches higher math and technology at a local public high school. He's a popular teacher with years of experience.

One of the courses he teaches is Discrete Math, which teaches students to apply math in a wide variety of subjects, such as math and physics, or math and biology. Grades for this public school class are based on the following factors:

- 60 percent is based on tests
- 25 percent is based on class participation
- 15 percent is based on homework

He also uses a common grading scale: 93-100 is an *A*, 90-92 is an *A-*, etc. He grades on the curve and tells his students, "Each chapter test will be worth one hundred points and I reserve the right to curve tests and lower the test value." For example, if 75 percent was the highest on a test, then everybody would receive 25 percent added to their test, so the person who earned 50 percent on the test would get an additional 25, bringing their final score to 75 percent on the test.

This teacher also has an open-book policy. Any homework or notes students have taken can be used during the test. In our homeschool, when my sons took their tests, I went grocery shopping and took the answer key with me. A couple of chapters in biology were so difficult that I resorted to open book tests.

My nephew also drops tests. If his students show up on time and hand in outstanding homework, they can drop their lowest test. I also offered this option to my children. Everybody has a bad day now and then, including children. When they went to college (at a private university), all of my children's professors allowed them to drop their lowest test score, so you can feel completely comfortable dropping the lowest test score if you wish.

My nephew's policy is to provide one make-up opportunity per test. Because this is done in public schools, you can feel comfortable giving your children an opportunity to re-take a test, too!

How Random Teachers Grade

Recently, I visited a school website with 48 different class syllabuses. I looked over each one and was astonished by the variety of grading criteria used. In these 48 classes, there seemed to be 48 ways to grade! One of the history classes graded only through tests and quizzes, which I thought would have probably killed me if I had been in the class. One P.E. class only based grades on participation (1/2 the grade) and physical skills (1/2 the grade). Almost all of the syllabuses provided bonus points for simply showing up to class. Many of them had my most common grading scale of 90 to 100 percent for an *A*.

On the same website, I found great course titles. Some of the more unusual course titles were:

- Relationships, Career, and Family
- Clothing and Apparel Management
- Child Development and Parenting
- Business Principles and Applications

- Word Processing

The grading criteria for Word Processing was based on typing using the home keys (60 percent), taking timed tests during typing (20 percent), and assignments which you took home and brought back to school (20 percent).

Again, the point here is to notice the variation in grading methods and criteria. So many homeschool parents think there is only one right (rigorous) way to grade their children, when the reality is that grading is subjective.

Don't fall into the trap of letting someone else's expectations and beliefs dictate how you evaluate your children. You know your children best and are the best person to evaluate them. Give them grades that are fair and true, based on your knowledge of their performance and abilities.

Chapter 5

Grading Papers

Many homeschool parents freak out about grading their children's English papers. Writing is so subjective, right? (I always wonder what e. e. cummings' English teacher wrote on his high school English papers). Instead of stressing about grading their writing, remember that you are striving to teach your children to write. It's okay to circle different problems on an essay for correction without putting a grade, percentile, or number system on it. Simply circle the word in a question and ask, "Is this word correct?" or "Did you spell this word correctly?" In the same way, you can circle any problems or sections you don't understand.

Our Homeschool

My son loved economics and wrote about economics all the time, whereas I failed economics in school. When I was in college, I got a 0.7 my first time through economics, and I frankly did not understand anything my son said. When we graded his papers, my husband and I would circle any problems and say, "I don't understand this. Could you please clarify?" The important point about writing is to learn to communicate clearly. If your student can't explain something clearly to a grown adult, then perhaps they should rewrite their essay.

In our homeschool, we circled changes to be made and asked our children to make corrections. Sometimes this went back and forth twice, and occasionally three times, but we let them correct the papers. When they were all done, we said "Good job," and gave them 100 percent for their English paper. This is exactly how their college professors marked papers when they got to their honors classes in college. They circled the errors, allowed the correction, and then graded the final paper.

Ratio-of-Annoyance

If grading papers is stressful, I'd like to offer you my trademark "Ratio-of-Annoyance" technique. Here's how this simple technique works:

1. When your student turns in their project, if you're not annoyed at all, go ahead and give them 100 percent for the assignment.

2. If you feel particularly picky, you might give them 95 percent.

3. If you feel they did a good job but could do more, give them 90 percent.

4. If they didn't do extremely well, but probably better than some public school kids and you're glad

you're homeschooling so you can correct it, but you're still not completely happy, then give them 80 percent.

The HomeScholar Factor of Confidence

I have another method of grading assignments, which I call "The HomeScholar Factor of Confidence."

1. If your child meets your high expectations, then give them an *A*.

2. If your child is doing well but not great, give them a *B*.

3. If your child is not doing well at all, but still moving onto the next level, and seems to be doing all right with it, then give them a *C*.

4. If they're somewhere in-between, you can certainly throw a dart on a number. If it's not quite an *A* but certainly better than a *B*, then you can give them a *B+*, or if you feel

it's not worthy of an *A* but it certainly wasn't *B* work, then you can give them an *A-*.

The Final Outcome

Grading papers is like making sausage. It's a messy process, like learning how to write, and it doesn't come out perfectly when you're working on it. You wouldn't want to assign a grade during the process of making sausage; it's better to wait until it's fully cooked and in the bun. The same is true about evaluating your child's writing.

I often point people to the book *501 Writing Prompts* for grading papers. It gives some useful help for evaluating daily work. Along with writing prompts, it shows what each kind of paper should look like. There are examples of a perfect paper, a moderately good paper, and a rotten paper.

See Appendix 1 for more information about how you can use your level of annoyance as a tool for grading.

Chapter 6

Determining Class Grades

When you're determining grades for your student's transcript, make sure each grade includes all the ways you evaluated them and not just their test scores. If you grade solely on tests, you are putting your child at a disadvantage when compared to all the other kids in public and private schools.

In high schools, as well as some colleges, students may never be judged based on test scores alone. After all, a test only measures what you *don't* know. We are trying to express what our children *do* know. A grade is usually a mix of criteria and if we don't grade with a mix as well, we are putting our kids at a disadvantage.

As homeschoolers, we tend to move on after our kids have mastered the material. If you send math problems, English papers, or tests back to your student with "please correct this" messages, then you have high expectations. I recommend giving your student 100 percent for each test or assignment that meets your expectations. If it means you're giving them a 4.0 in every class, that's fine, as long as they meet your high expectations.

Grading Criteria

When I was homeschooling, I graded each course my students took using two or three separate criteria. One third of their grade was based on the first criteria, another third for the second criteria, and a final one third for the last criteria. I then took all two or three areas and averaged them for a final grade. Other homeschoolers feel comfortable assigning points; they might give fifty points for every test and ten points for every quiz.

You can give a grade for every test, quiz, paper, or lab report. But I encourage you to include other non-test-related methods, such as independent reading, reports, discussion, research, daily work, oral presentation, composition, practice, performance, note taking, attendance, and narration. You may want to give a grade for each activity your child completes within a course. For example, you could give a grade for every activity you count for P.E. hours: swim team, skiing, soccer, free weights, health, and softball. For music, you might want to give a grade for lessons, practice, and performance. In history, you could give a separate grade for each report, paper, or essay they write.

I kept traditional grades in biology, mostly because the curriculum provided tests. Even so, my students did more for that course than merely take a test, and I wanted this reflected in their grade. I supplied a numerical percentage grade for each test, grading as suggested by the curriculum supplier.

The other major activity in the course was their science lab. I decided to give them a grade for every science lab completed. If they met expectations, their grade was 100 percent. They didn't always meet my expectations, however. When my kids did a lab write-up, I expected them to give me a paragraph describing what they did, along with a diagram, chart, or sketch of the experiment. There were times I felt they hadn't done their best. I sometimes gave them 80 or 90 percent, depending on my mood. Yes, it was arbitrary! But they had *not* met my expectations and I wanted their grade to reflect this.

Homeschool 4.0

"Mom knows best" sometimes means a grade will be a *B* or lower. When you honestly know your child has performed at a lower than *A* level, don't be afraid about how it will look on a transcript. Honesty will always serve our children best, and a *B* can demonstrate thoughtful consideration of your grades. It says all your grades are real and you have considered each one carefully. There are times when your honest grade will include a *B* (or lower) on a test or paper.

Make sure the total grade on the transcript accurately reflects everything your student does, and every area you evaluate their work. If they have earned an *A* for effort in a variety of criteria (discussion, daily work, narration, research, lab work) be sure to include everything they do. In the end, if the transcript grade is still less than an *A* then go ahead and write it down. There is no permanent damage! If it's honest, write it down.

My grading system is one of many *right ways* to do things. As the parent, you can decide the "right way" to grade your homeschool. I'm giving you this glimpse into my homeschool evaluation methods because I think it helps to see what someone else has done. This is only for you to consider and adapt for yourself. When I started thinking about transcripts, I loved seeing every sample I could find!

At times it's appropriate to show the nuances of your grades to a college, and you want to demonstrate that your homeschool 4.0 is not a number pulled out of thin air. Demonstrate thoughtful consideration of the ways you evaluated your student. You want to show your standards and your method of grading. Then let the college decide how they will use the grades, knowing you did your best to provide them with the information they need.

Homeschool grading is an art, not a science. Don't feel like you have to do everything exactly the way I did. Mom and Dad know best—especially when it comes to how to evaluate their own children.

Chapter 7

What About Weighting Grades?

I don't recommend weighting grades. The problem is that every high school has a different policy on weighting grades. This makes it harder for colleges, and colleges like you more when you make their job easier.

For an Honors or AP class, some high schools add 1.0 to the grade so that the highest grade possible is a 5.0 instead of a 4.0. Some high schools increase the grade by 0.5, so honors classes can earn a 4.5 grade. To further complicate things, some high schools change the credit value. An honors class might be worth 2.0 credits or 1.5 credits, instead of the normal 1.0 credit. There are so many possibilities and colleges need to compare students from different schools and school districts. For this reason, the first thing they do is un-weight any weighted grades. Colleges have asked me to tell parents not to weight grades, so I never recommend weighting grades unless your first choice college prefers weighting.

High schools weight grades so their student population looks smarter and more college ready. It sounds great in their marketing materials to say their average GPA at school is 3.2, when they don't have to mention how many kids earned 5.0 grades. High schools do it for marketing purposes but it's not helpful for colleges.

However, public schools do weight grades sometimes, and each school or school district can have their own grading policy. As a homeschooler, you can decide on your own school policy on weighting grades. If you do decide to weight your grades, look over these options and decide what's best for you.

Here are the easiest ways I have seen for weighting grades for honors or AP classes:

- Credit: double the credit value of the class to 2.0
- Credit: increase the credit value of the class to 1.5
- Grade: add 1.0 to your final grade
- Grade: add 0.5 to your final grade

Other high schools have a grading scale specific to honors level courses, like this:

Grade Points awarded

- A (90-100%) 5.00
- B (80-89%) 3.75
- C (70-79%) 2.50
- D (60-69%) 1.25

- F (0-59%) 0.00

Some high schools don't increase the value of the class, instead adding to the grade point average after it has been calculated. In other words, they calculate the GPA first, then add a bonus credit for each honors class. Here is an example from Virginia Beach public schools:

Bonus Credit for Year-long Honors Level Course

- A, A- add to the GPA .0488

- B+, B, B- add to the GPA .0366

- C+, C, C- add to the GPA .0244

- D+, D add to the GPA .0122

- E add to the GPA 0

Some high schools will weight grades differently depending on the class. For example, Weston High School weights their grades using a complicated multi-variable scale:

- AP classes can earn 5.0
- Honors classes can earn 4.7
- College prep classes earn the regular 4.0
- Foundations (remedial) classes can earn a 3.0

	Advanced Placement	Honors	College Prep	Foundations
A	5.0	4.7	4.0	3.0
A-	4.7	4.4	3.7	2.7
B+	4.3	4.0	3.3	2.3
B	4.0	3.7	3.0	2.0
B-	3.7	3.4	2.7	1.7
C+	3.3	3.0	2.3	1.3
C	3.0	2.7	2.0	1.0
C-	2.7	2.4	1.7	.7
D=	2.3	2.0	1.3	.3
D	2.0	1.7	1.0	0
D-	1.7	1.4	.7	0
F	0	0	0	0

It's not only honors classes, either. Some high schools give a 4.3 for perfect grades in regular courses:

- A+ = 4.3 GPA
- A = 4 GPA
- A- = 3.7 GPA
- B+ = 3.3 GPA
- B = 3 GPA
- B- = 2.7 GPA
- C+ = 2.3 GPA
- C = 2 GPA
- C- = 1.7 GPA
- D+ = 1.3 GPA
- D = 1 GPA
- D- = 0.7 GPA
- F = 0 GPA

You can see how complicated weighted grades could be to a college comparing different students from school districts all across the nation, all of whom have differently weighted grades. It's a big problem for colleges!

Here is the bottom line; I find weighting grades to be incredibly complicated for no perceivable difference in college admission and scholarships. For this reason, I do not recommend weighting grades.

Conclusion

Learning is More Important than Grades

In the long run, real learning and values are more important than grades. You want your child to learn how to learn and ultimately succeed in life. When your child gets out into the real world they will need to know that grading is subjective. I know it feels uncomfortable to be the mom, knowing your grades are subjective, but it's important to remember that if they were in public or private school, their teachers would grade subjectively as well. It's not as if you're the only one who is subjective; all grading is subjective!

Now that my children are out of college, it's interesting to see what really matters in terms of success in college. College grades have more to do with hard work; it's a matter of turning in assignments and doing the work, not about perfection. One of my children is a perfectionist who struggled with college because he didn't want to turn in anything that wasn't perfect. He sometimes turned things in late and got lower grades as a result. In college, turning it in on time matters more than perfection.

Success in college also has to do with values. When kids go to college to learn, they will have to decide for themselves whether they are going to drink and party instead. Real learning and real values will help your child succeed in college. These will matter, long after the transcript has been forgotten.

Resources

GPA Conversion Charts

How to Convert Your GPA to a 4.0 Scale

(Reference: collegeboard.com/html/academicTracker-howtoconvert.html)

Colleges report GPA (grade point average) on a 4.0 scale. The top grade is an *A*, which equals 4.0. This is the standard scale at most colleges, and many high schools use it.

If your high school uses a different or weighted system, you need to convert your GPA to a 4.0 scale for this tool.

College Board Conversion Chart

A+   (97-100)   = 4.0

A-   (93-96)   = 4.0

A-   (90-92)   = 3.7

B+ - (87-89)   = 3.3

B   (83-86)   = 3.0

B-   (80-82)   = 2.7

C+   (77-79)   = 2.3

C   (73-76)   = 2.0

C-   (70-72)   = 1.7

D+   (67-69)   = 1.3

D   (65-66)   = 1.0

E/F (below 65) = 0.0

Princeton Review GPA Conversion Chart

GPA	Percentile	Letter Grade
4.0	95-100	A
3.9	94	A
3.8	93	A
3.7	92	A
3.6	91	A
3.5	90	A
3.4	89	B
3.3	88	B
3.2	87	B
3.1	86	B

3.0	85	B
2.9	84	B
2.8	83	B
2.7	82	B
2.6	81	B
2.5	80	B
2.4	79	C
2.3	78	C
2.2	77	C
2.1	76	C
2.0	75	C
1.9	74	C

Making the Grades

1.8	73	C
1.7	72	C
1.6	71	C
1.5	70	C
1.4	69	D
1.3	68	D
1.2	67	D
1.1	66	D
1.0	65	D
0.9	65	D
0.8	65	D
0.7	65	D

0.6	65	D
0.5	65	D
0.4	65	F
0.3	65	F
0.2	65	F
0.1	65	F

Appendix 1

The Annoyed Mom's Guide to Grading

Confessions of a homeschool mom . . . I sometimes felt annoyed with my children. My son, Kevin, seemed to always be playing chess, no matter what I said or did! To this day, I still feel annoyance swell up every time I hear a chess piece clunk down on a table. It makes me feel like someone should be helping me by setting the table or doing anything other than playing chess.

When I was homeschooling, it seemed I could hear Alex banging away at the piano every time I turned around. Certain classical pieces still have pet names in our family. The "frantic plumber song" (A.K.A. Mozart's "Ronda Alla Turca") earned the name because it seemed to always be playing in the background during a plumbing crisis.

Sometimes, it wasn't so much the noise, but the silence. The sound of silence usually meant Alex was reading an economics book instead of working on his math tutorial.

Use Your Annoy-O-Meter Skillfully

I can't tell you how many times I said, "Stop playing chess!" or "Put that book down!" When a child finds their passion, they pursue it with all their heart and soul and it can be annoying to Mom! We watch them *waste away* spending time on their interests, instead of pursuing things *we* value. It's a challenge to keep *their* specialization *our* top priority.

I know I am not alone. One of my clients has a son who is gifted in music. She said to me, "But it's not real music, it's just bluegrass." She was doing *exactly* what I had done with chess and economics! Of *course* bluegrass is real music! But it can be hard to support and encourage things we don't understand.

Being annoyed is . . . annoying! But it can also be helpful! No, I'm not kidding. You can use your feelings of frustration to help you determine what to include on the high school transcript.

I suppose annoyance is less of a homeschooling thing and more of a parenting thing. But what we *say* when we are annoyed can help us with high school record keeping. Listen carefully to what you say when you are annoyed with your child and you might get some informational clues for their transcript. I don't want to assume for a moment, however, that *you* are ever annoyed at your child! But here is what *my* annoyance meant to *me*.

Scenario 1: Annoyance Can Demonstrate Specialization

Colleges look for passion in kids. For some reason (God's sense of humor, perhaps?) activities kids are passionate about seem to frequently frustrate parents. In terms of my own home, let me show you how this played out. Mom says, "Will you *please* put that down and do your work?" With Kevin, *that* was a chess piece. For Alex, *that* was usually an economics book.

It's hard to recognize specialization when it is so much fun for our students, too. Shouldn't they be working? They're only having *fun*! If you are struggling with specialization, remember colleges love to see passion. They see unique specialization in homeschoolers and they love it!

What does your child do that drives you nuts? Could it be their specialization . . . an interest they are passionate about?

Now, I'll admit sometimes it can be merely them wasting time, but if they are actively engaged in an activity, what is it? Put aside your pre-conceived notions about which interests are valuable.

I notice parents sometimes see their child's faults easier than they see their strengths. A gift is something children engage in repeatedly, to the point of annoyance! Check yourself the next time you feel annoyed with your child. What are they doing when you say "Will you knock that off!?" Ask yourself if you are looking at one of their gifts. I know parents who have pooh-poohed some wonderful activities they thought didn't have any value. Some parents didn't think an activity was academic enough and others thought it was too narrow. Some have dismissed an interest because it wasn't a college-level interest, merely "messing around on the computer" with programming languages. So put aside your bias and listen to what you say when you are annoyed. Ask yourself, "Could it be their area of specialization?"

Scenario 2: Annoyance Can Be included on a High School Transcript!

Things that bother us often become our subconscious grading criteria. Our frustrations can indicate what course work we have assigned. Think about this statement: "Aren't you done with your spelling words *yet*?" It indicates you consider spelling part of their English class. Or what about this, "Is that all you want to read about?" This could demonstrate the child is working on a delight directed course, learning without any assignments at all! Can you figure out a course name for this delight?

Then there is the classic phrase, "You simply *have* to put that down now and do some school!" This statement can help you determine credit value for your delight directed course. How often do you say it? Once a week? Once a day? Once an hour? This may mean your child is spending more than five hours a week on the activity and you might be able to make it a high school credit. (Yes, I know for some kids it's more like five hours per day)!

Scenario 3: Annoyance Can Indicate College Credits

Sometimes a child will annoy us with a skill that can be measured. If your child has an interest in an academic subject, consider getting their knowledge assessed. Even if you aren't *teaching* the class, the student may still be learning material because they are interested. This happened to me with my economics-loving son. I realized I was annoyed with his economics study, so I thought I should probably include it on his transcript. Although it felt like he read economics all day, every day, I felt too unsure of myself to give him a whole credit. On his transcript, I decided to write Economics 1, Economics 2, and Economics 3 with a half credit value each. Then I thought perhaps he could pass an economics exam.

This turned out to be a fateful decision. I discovered through CLEP exams that he knew a college amount of information about economics (and other topics I never taught him at all)! Based on those test results, I revised his transcript. I awarded one credit in economics, one credit in macroeconomics, and one credit in microeconomics. I gave him honors for all three classes. The CLEP exam provided information about class titles, grades, and credit value. If your child has an academic interest, look into SAT Subject Tests, AP exams, or CLEP tests to see if their annoying interest can be measured as college credit.

Scenario 4: Annoyance Can Be Included on an Activity and Award List

Some annoying activities core but are more extracurricular. If your child competes or receives honors in an area they love, put it on the activity and award list. Sometimes parents will laugh a little, and say, "You're not going to believe this but he actually won _____ award." Or perhaps the child has sold his band CDs or won a huge cash prize for playing "Halo" (I know both of these kids). Or, like my Kevin, perhaps they win chess tournaments!

All of these can go on their activity and award list and the more the better! Colleges love passion, which means they love to see a *lot* of one interest over all four years of high school. We may want our kids to be well rounded (I know I did!) but it also helps for them to have activities they engage in consistently. Lacrosse, youth group, or Eagle Scouts for four years. When it comes to applying for college, four years of an activity is ten times better than one year!

Scenario 5: Annoyance Can Indicate Career Preparation

As your child grows, often their interests change. Yes, passion for a subject during all four years of high school is great, but you also want to expose them to *many* interests so the student can shape their ideas about a career. My son Alex loves playing the piano, but after years of playing he realized he liked it *for fun* but didn't want piano to be his career. You can let them change interests and move their focus from one activity to the next.

It can be amazing when they put all the pieces of the puzzle together. As a senior in high school, my son Kevin couldn't decide on a college major. Finally, he decided chess involved problem solving and electrical engineering also involved problem solving plus a lot of math! He won awards in math competitions as well as winning chess tournaments. He decided to be an engineer because of his interest in chess and math. Each activity seemed isolated until he put them together, with a straight line pointing to his college major and career interest! Encouraging specialization, even when it changes, can ultimately help with career choices.

"OK, I'm annoyed! What do I do now?"

- Use the information on their transcript. Let your frustrations be your guide for course titles, grades, credit values, and activity lists.

- Encourage their interests, as long as they're actively involved in them and not merely laziness. Feed into their passionate pursuits.

- On The HomeScholar website at www.homehighschoolhelp.com, you can find the article, "Christmas Presents that Pay for College." Read it over before you do Christmas shopping.

- If your child loves an academic area, consider taking their interest to the next level with college level lectures from The Great Courses.

Appendix 2

The HomeScholar Answers Parents' Questions

Here are questions I've answered that were asked by real homeschool parents on the topic of grading.

Question: *I grade elementary tests and upper level grades. I always start with great ideals but not so much towards the end. I like grading because it verifies my instinct. What do you think about this?*

Answer: I talk about this at conventions. Sometimes a parent will say, "I really think that my child is going to get an *A* but I really don't feel comfortable giving them an *A*, so I'm going to go over every last thing that they did." Then the mom will go over every single paper and discover her instinct was correct. I do see that as good validation, but I don't think you necessarily have to go through all of that.

Question: *Can you explain averaging accumulative GPA for future transcripts?*

Answer: To calculate the GPA for your transcript, you have to calculate the grade points for each class. To do this, take the grade for the class, such as a 4.0 grade, then multiply by the credits for that class, so a half credit class would end up with 2 grade points.

Every one credit class that has a 4.0 would get 4 grade points and every half credit class that has a 4.0 would get 2 grade points. That's why you assign grade points for every single class on your transcript. Then add all of the grade points together on your transcript and divide that number by the total number of credits with a grade on your transcript.

Alternately, I found the grade point average for my homeschool by simply making sure that my children had to get a 90 percent or better so that I could give them a 4.0. and then I never had to calculate the GPA.

Question: *Is it okay to grade assignments with a letter grade or no points associated?*

Answer: Yes, that's exactly what I did. Much of the time when we graded English papers or projects, my husband and I would put a general *A*, *A-*, or *B+* on a particular assignment.

Question: *How early should we begin grading?*

Answer: When I was homeschooling, I tried to teach myself how to keep grades when my children were in 7th and 8th grades. I kept grades for all their tests and papers starting in 7th grade. Ultimately, when one of my children ended up graduating early, I was so glad I did this because I needed every single grade I'd written down. If you look closely at some of my early high school credits in my children's comprehensive records, you'll see that I lost some of the tests and I didn't write them down. I do recommend that you start in 7th or 8th grade at least for practice, but it certainly counts in 9th grade.

Question: *Did your sons go away to college or did they go to a local college?*

Answer: When my children were seniors in high school, they went to the community college for one year of dual enrollment. I do consider this to have been a mistake; both of my children have told me it was a mistake but we certainly do have some experiences to talk about. If you're interested in why community college wasn't so great for us, you can go to The HomeScholar blog at www.homehighschoolhelp.com/blogs and search for "community college stories."

Question: *How can you use the Dave Ramsey finance series as a class?*

Answer: Quite a few of my clients have used this for a personal economics class. Because I'm so fond of economics since my son was so involved in it, I might supplement with the *Whatever Happened to Penny Candy?* book, possibly with a workbook as a half credit economics class. Make sure to read the book first before assigning it, to make sure it is consistent with your worldview.

There are many daily hands-on projects for Dave Ramsey; it's quite time consuming, so additional class work may not be necessary. When we were working on one of my client's transcripts, we called the class "Introduction to Personal Finance in Economics."

Question: *What about the Word Smart series for vocabulary building?*

Answer: I would probably include it within your English class, with Word Smart making sure you evaluate every assignment.

Question: *How do you grade if you unschool?*

Answer: You can evaluate your child in different ways by having them take a CLEP, an AP, or SAT Subject Tests. Or you can put down the titles of classes you have seen them unschool, then give them grades based on the annoyance I talked about. If they met your high expectations in ornithology, then you may award them 100 percent.

Question: *Is it OK to go into detail on how you evaluated your students on the course descriptions?*

Answer: That's exactly what I did. When I wrote course descriptions, I recorded every single way I evaluated them, even though they didn't include testing.

Question: *I get confused on all the different grading criteria out there.*

Answer: I think it's important to know that every grading scale is different. On my Gold Care Club membership site, there is a section called Grading Criteria with a wide variety to choose from. Teachers each get to choose their own grading scales and some of them will use different numbers so a 90 percent might be a different grade for different grading criteria.

Question: *When figuring out a cumulative GPA, do you take the total from 9th and 10th grades and average them?*

Answer: Yes. When you're doing a cumulative GPA, you do the whole thing for every class completed. You don't divide by the number of credits they're in the process of completing. Don't calculate a GPA for 9th grade and then

10th grade and then average those averages. Instead, you should do the whole transcript as one gigantic piece, adding up all the grade points and dividing by all the credits.

Some schools segment out their GPA and say, "I got a GPA of 3.0 in 9th grade and a GPA of 4.0 in 10th grade." When you're calculating the accumulative GPA, you do so for the transcript as a whole instead of dividing it. One of the reasons why I didn't include a GPA for each of the years of school is because I found that completely overwhelming and opted not to do so.

Question: *When you talk about credits, how do you know how many credits a class is worth?*

Answer: In general, if you're using a textbook then you count credits with the textbook first. Usually the textbook will count as a whole credit unless it's a semester class, then the textbook is half a credit. As soon as your child is done, give them a whole credit or half credit based on the text.

If you're counting credit for something like P.E. or art by counting hours, then a whole credit is 120 to 180 hours of work.

Question: *Do you take all three years total and average them together?*

Answer: It does make a little bit of difference. You don't want to average 9th grade, average 10th grade, average 11th grade, and then average those three years together. When you determine a cumulative GPA, you take all 24 classes on the transcript and find the cumulative grade point average for the whole thing. My engineer husband taught me never to average averages!

Question: *Did you create a separate English literature class using Sonlight?*

Answer: Yes, I did. When you use Sonlight, it will be one credit of history, one credit of English, and probably a half a credit of Bible studies.

Question: *How did you grade Sonlight literature?*

Answer: I created one column with an evaluation based on standardized tests that covered mechanics, spelling, usage, and punctuation.

Another 1/3 grade for their Sonlight was based on reading. It was research reading and book reading; you could even give them a grade for each book they read if you want to get into detail. If they read the book to your high expectations, you could give them 100 percent. Remember that public schools might base their grades on turning in homework.

The final 1/3 was based on their writing. In some years, I listed the kinds of writing they did, such as poetry, research writing, and short essays. In other years, I listed the grades for the topics of papers they wrote, such as the Civil War, the Revolutionary War, and George Washington.

Question: *One of my sons is participating in a local fire department cadet program. How can I use and grade that participation?*

Answer: Without knowing exactly what he's doing, it's hard to say. Sometimes they'll tell you what they're learning each day, and you can put it into groups like teaching first aid. This would be part of your child's P.E. class.

Other experiences might include an internship or occupational education. When dealing with a work skill, my default position is to put it down as occupational education. That's something I recommend especially in my home state of Washington because it is one of the classes required for homeschool graduation. You can call it "Fire Department Internship" or "Fire Department Cadet Internship."

Simply count hours. When you get to 120 to 180 hours working as a fire department cadet, then you can call it one credit and give that achievement grade when he meets your high expectations by showing up, doing the work, and getting positive feedback.

Question: *How many credits do you give for a CLEP test or community college? Do you use the grade already* *given since the college level grade is raised?*

Answer: You can do it any way you want. When your children go to college, their transcript will be dissected and reevaluated by the college you send it to. Whether you weight grades or not, if you use a 4.0 or 5.0 scale, or you give more or the same credits for AP classes, it really won't matter because the college will readjust it later.

If you want to elevate their grades, you can probably do so. Personally, I did not find this to be particularly useful. My children earned good grades at community college and I didn't want them to look more elevated. I guess I tried to look humble as if I was expecting them to get good grades.

Every time my children passed a CLEP test, I gave them 1.0 credit, called the class exactly the name of the CLEP test, and I gave them an *A*. I did this every time they passed with a 50 or above on the CLEP because it demonstrated a college amount of learning. Somebody at the convention asked me why my child had 11 credits one year of high school. When she showed me this on my child's homeschool records, I was mortified because I tell my Gold Care members not to teach so many classes and burn their kids out.

When I looked at it more closely, I realized that was the year my children had taken all their CLEP tests. When they passed a CLEP, I added it onto their transcript even though they hadn't been studying for it and it wasn't planned.

When they take a community college class, make sure you take the grade the college gave you and put the same grade on your child's transcript. One of the things that will do is provide validation that your grades are true.

Question: *What about community college credits?*

Answer: For community college credit, every time your child takes a full class at a community college, it is equal to one whole high school credit. If your community college is on semesters, then a five or six credit semester class will be one whole credit. Each successful CLEP exam can be counted as one whole high school credit.

Question: *Is it okay to grade courses differently? For one year, you grade individual papers and then another year you list types of papers. Would it look bad in course descriptions?*

Answer: No, I think this is fine. You need to remember that chart with 48 different teachers' 48 grading criteria. If you had 48 different classes in your homeschool and 48 ways of evaluating, it would be perfectly fine.

Afterword

Who is Lee Binz and What Can She Do for Me?

Number one best-selling homeschool author, Lee Binz is The HomeScholar. Her mission is "helping parents homeschool high school." Lee and her husband, Matt, homeschooled their two boys, Kevin and Alex, from elementary through high school.

Upon graduation, both boys received four-year, full tuition scholarships from their first choice university. This enables Lee to pursue her dream job—helping parents homeschool their children through high school.

On The HomeScholar website, you will find great products for creating homeschool transcripts and comprehensive records to help you amaze and impress colleges.

Find out why Andrew Pudewa, Founder of the Institute for Excellence in Writing says, "Lee Binz knows how to navigate this often confusing and frustrating labyrinth better than anyone."

You can find Lee online at:

HomeHighSchoolHelp.com

If this book has been helpful, could you please take a minute to write us a quick review on Amazon? Thank you!

Testimonials

My Personal HomeScholar Tutor!

Hi Lee!!!

Haven't contacted you since my senior, Bryan, was accepted into the University of North Carolina School of the Arts in April! I understand that they interviewed him with his "Comprehensive High School Record" open in their possession, referring to details within it during the interview! Wow—what fun to know that all that work was of value to them in their job of selecting candidates for their program. Thank you, Lee, for the unspeakably big help you were in that whole process of my documenting his high school years!

I had done NO course descriptions until I started fall of last year!! Nightmare! But your help and guidance got me through it beautifully (although exhausted) in time to submit it all in December! Well—my rising 10th and 11th graders are NOT going to be in the same place by the time THEIR applications are rolling—this mom's got some SERIOUS templates to work from, and multitudes of know-how, thanks to my personal HomeScholar tutor!"

~ Mary, homeschool mom to Bryan

Very Professional and Detailed

Hi Lee,

Once again, I thank you from the bottom of my heart for everything you've done for me and my family, even in a month's worth of time. I am so happy with your Total Transcript Solution; we can definitely home school through high school! You, and the products you've put together, give practical help and encouragement like no one else. I keep reading your blog. I keep mentioning you and your site to homeschooling friends. Thank you and keep it up!!!"

~ Christina in New York City.

For more information about my **Total Transcript Solution** and **Comprehensive Record Solution**, go to:

www.TotalTranscriptSolution.com and www.ComprehensiveRecordSolution.com

Also From The HomeScholar...

- The HomeScholar Guide to College Admission and Scholarships: Homeschool Secrets to Getting Ready, Getting In and Getting Paid (Book and Kindle Book)

- Setting the Records Straight—How to Craft Homeschool Transcripts and Course Descriptions for College Admission and Scholarships (Book and Kindle Book)

- TechnoLogic: How to Set Logical Technology Boundaries and Stop the Zombie Apocalypse

- Finding the Faith to Homeschool

High School

- Parent Training A la Carte (Online Training)

- Total Transcript Solution (Online Training, Tools, and Templates)

- Comprehensive Record Solution (Online Training, Tools, and Templates)

- High School Solution (Online Training, Tools, Resources, and Support)

- College Launch Solution (Online Training, Tools, Resources, and Support)

- Gold Care Club (Comprehensive Online Support and Training)

- Silver Training Club (Online Training)

- The HomeScholar Bookshelf (Collection of Print Books)

The HomeScholar Coffee Break Books Released or Coming Soon on Kindle and Paperback:

- Delight Directed Learning: Guiding Your Homeschooler Toward Passionate Learning

- Creating Transcripts for Your Unique Child: Help Your Homeschool Graduate Stand Out from the Crowd

- Beyond Academics: Preparation for College and for Life

- Planning High School Courses: Charting the Course Toward High School Graduation

- Graduate Your Homeschooler in Style: Make Your Homeschool Graduation Memorable

- Keys to High School Success: Get Your Homeschool High School Started Right!

- Getting the Most Out of Your Homeschool This Summer: Learning just for the Fun of it!

- Finding a College: A Homeschooler's Guide to Finding a Perfect Fit

- College Scholarships for High School Credit: Learn and Earn With This Two-for-One Strategy!

- College Admission Policies Demystified: Understanding Homeschool Requirements for Getting In

- A Higher Calling: Homeschooling High School for Harried Husbands (by Matt Binz, Mr. HomeScholar)

- Gifted Education Strategies for Every Child: Homeschool Secrets for Success

- College Application Essays: A Primer for Parents

- Creating Homeschool Balance: Find Harmony Between Type A and Type Zzz...

- Homeschooling the Holidays: Sanity Saving Strategies and Gift Giving Ideas

- Your Goals this Year: A Year by Year Guide to Homeschooling High School

- Making the Grades: A Grouch-Free Guide to Homeschool Grading

- High School Testing: Knowledge That Saves Money

- Getting the BIG Scholarships: Learn Expert Secrets for Winning College Cash!

- Easy English for Simple Homeschooling: How to Teach, Assess and Document High School English

- Scheduling — The Secret to Homeschool Sanity: Plan You Way Back to Mental Health

- Junior Year is the Key to High School Success: How to Unlock the Gate to Graduation and Beyond

- Upper Echelon Education: How to Gain Admission to Elite Universities

- How to Homeschool College: Save Time, Reduce Stress and Eliminate Debt

- Homeschool Curriculum That's Effective and Fun: Avoid the Crummy Curriculum Hall of Shame!

- Comprehensive Homeschool Records: Put Your Best Foot Forward to Win College Admission and Scholarships

- Options After High School: Steps to Success for College or Career

- How to Homeschool 9th and 10th Grade: Simple Steps for Starting Strong!

- Senior Year Step-by-Step: Simple Instructions for Busy Homeschool Parents

- How-to-Homeschool Independently: Do-it-Yourself Secrets to Rekindle the Love of Learning

- High School Math The Easy Way: Simple Strategies for Homeschool Parents in Over Their Heads

- Homeschooling Middle School with Powerful Purpose: How to Successfully Navigate 6th through 8th Grade

- Simple Science for Homeschooling High School: Because Teaching Science isn't Rocket Science!

Would you like to be notified when we offer the next Coffee Break Books for FREE during our Kindle promotion days? If so, leave your name and email below and we will send you a reminder.

HomeHighSchoolHelp.com/freekindlebook

Visit my Amazon Author Page!

amazon.com/author/leebinz

Made in the USA
Lexington, KY
02 November 2018